Made of Stones

Ade Couper

Made of Stories
Ade Couper
Edited by Black Pear Press

First published in 2023 by Black Pear Press
www.blackpear.net
Copyright © Ade Couper

ISBN 978-1-913418-92-2

Cover image by Tony Judge & DALL·E 2
Cover design by Black Pear Press

Black Pear Press

Dedication

Respectfully dedicated to the memory of my father, Kenneth Edwin Couper, and my grandfather, Ivor Stanley Moss.

Introduction

First of all, an apology—to anyone hoping to find the train toilets poem within, I'm afraid that's for another volume…

This collection is themed around ability: it includes poems from my perspective as a disabled person, and what it is like living with chronic health conditions. It also includes poems from my perspective as a health and social care professional who's worked in mental health care, as well as dementia support, for around 20 years, and also some pieces on how disability is seen—the 'political stuff' if you like.

My collection will hopefully give you some insight into living with a long-term health condition—you may laugh at some of the pieces and cry at others.

I make no apology for the fact that some of these pieces are hard-hitting: many of these pieces are ones that do face up to my own experience, and sometimes that's a lot to face.

I hope you enjoy this, my first collection—you can feed back to me on Twitter (@akc_0123) or Facebook 'Ade Couper'.

Contents

Diagnosis

August 2017: my dad
drives me to City Hospital
to get the final sentencing.

The consultant—tall, kind—asks me
to step into the treatment room
so he can pronounce my fate.

'We've had the results back from your tests:
I'm sorry to say I was right—
you are now living with M.S.'

I don't remember what I said
or how I felt—it's just a blank.
I do remember being led

by Dad back toward the car park,
but nothing of the journey home:
I don't think that I cried right then.

Made of Stories

The old squaddie who'd met Elvis
and had the photo with him still;
the woman stood at the bus stop
who'd been an extra in "The Bill";
the lonely old guy in his flat,
post left unnoticed on the mat,
memory waning, feeling bored—
he had helped to design Concorde.

The next-door neighbour—quiet, shy—
who'd helped the Thunderbirds to fly;
the old man, nearing end of life
mistakes his daughter for his wife;
the wartime pilot, all alone now,
if given chance, would tell you how
as well as fighting for the nation
he'd been a guard at the Coronation.

Everyone has a tale to tell,
some are exquisite, some are hell,
times and places that they have been,
those they have met, and what they've seen.
Some tales are too horrific to share,
most ignored by those who don't care—
but listen if you can, then please—
for we are all made of stories.

The Japanese have a Word for it...

He is broken—
physically, mentally, emotionally, and spiritually.
He has been broken so many, many times,
patched together
he is mosaic.

The Japanese have a word for it:
'Kintsugi',
the mending of broken crockery with gold.

The gold that repairs him
is the love of friends and family.
Worth far more than mere metal,
love freely given mends him
makes him whole again.

He could not be who he is,
do what he does,
without love.

Windfalls

Rotting on the ground,
shaken there by life's storms,
ignored, walked through by many:
'wonky', 'blemished',
not pretty enough for people—
considered second-class,
something you really shouldn't need
to put up with.

The fruit would be fine:
although the skin may be
bruised or blemished,
underneath it's fine.

Windfalls,
rotting on the ground.
Ignored.

The Creaking

Trapped inside a body that doesn't work,
struggling just to get through every day;
taking much longer to do everything,
knocking my confidence every which way
and more. Feeling my body is out of
my control; finding it really hard to say
'I need help'—admitting weakness isn't
easy, to ask for help isn't my way.

Feeling lost and lonely trapped inside me:
hobbling with a stick, I know you don't see
the man I was, or the man I could be.

I remember when life wasn't like this.

Won't You..?

Won't you push my chair for a mile?
I'm sure you'll do it in elegant style;
reflect on all those jokes you made,
as you push my chair for a mile.

Won't you walk with my stick a mile,
feel humiliation and bile?
You'll understand why I hate it so,
when you walk with my stick for a mile.

Won't you take my meds for a while?
You'll discover they are loathsome, vile;
the side-effects will make you ill
when you take my meds for a while.

Won't you live in my head a while?
The voices and demons damn and defile:
reflect on your taking the Mickey Bliss,
as you live in my head for a while.

The Dying Days

The mournful cries of the seagulls
echo my own melancholy;
like them, I would give anything
for open skies and empty seas.

'Progressive': it sounds positive,
makes you think of journeys and trips.
The reality is a sharp
clinical descent, which will strip
me of my dignity, maybe
my mind, my memories, my wits—
to say nothing of the loss of
physical skills, attributes: it's
a dark road ahead, wreathed in fog:
no idea what will happen, I'm
lost, scared, abandoned, in a bog,
a morass, blindly blundering—
and crapping myself, truth be told.
I remember The Who singing
"Hope I die before I get old"—
well, frankly, that's garbage, I do want
to get older. You value life
more when you know your time
is limited, just by a random act
of genetics; I don't want to
live forever, but not to hear
the clock always ticking would be
better—the silence of the tick
that's always there would just make
the time bearable. Still, that's the cards
I've been dealt, what will I gain
from whinging? You just have to
play your cards as best you can—doesn't
mean I have to like the game though.

I envy the seagulls. I wish
I could escape, and fly into
the open sky, floating over
empty ocean, master of my own destiny.
It's hard, being alone in a crowd,
where you see my stick,
you don't see me—
my disability is my
invisibility—having
now to use the priority
seating on the bus or the train;
thought of as a scrounger,
a cripple—no matter I'm a
poet, employed, an activist—
reduced to just a statistic,
not a real person anymore.

The grief, and the anger, sit well
with the pain and fear—knowing
things can only get worse, that this
is the best I'm going to be
for the rest of my life. However much I wish otherwise,
I've got it
and will use it to inspire me
to keep going as long
and as far as I can—my inner strength
goes into fighting this thing
even though I know I can't win.

I envy the seagulls.

Without Consent

"Do not attempt resuscitation"
seems self-explanatory
but could someone please explain to me
why our disabled brothers and sisters
are singled out, identified
as not worthy of living?
For far too many years
we have been seen
as not worth saving—
"Why bother, they have no quality of life"
is the subtext
from a medical establishment
that has loved to experiment
using us as guinea pigs.
I thought we'd got better than this—
but oh no—
scant years ago
in pandemic times
the medics declined
to see if we wanted
to be resuscitated.
Whatever happened to our human rights?
Just another oversight
where yet again
the facts remain
that, to them,
we are less than human.
We can do better than this
we can see something's amiss—
the establishment's taking the piss.
Our forebears fought hard
to get us where we are
and, for the most part, it's better by far
than before.

So, why still use D.N.A.R.
without our consent?
Are our lives meant
to be worth less?
Worthless?
We can do better than this.

Dear M.S.

Dear M.S.,
So, the other day I saw the nurse,
who confirmed that you're progressing
and that I am getting slowly worse.
It's not a surprise, to be fair:
I get that 'progressive' means
you will get the upper hand
eventually.

Though it seems
written in stone, just know this:
you may be taking my body
and my mind,
but my will, my heart
—they are still mine—
and you know what? I am going
to fight you every bloody inch
of the way—these heels will dig in.

You do your damnedest
to shatter my heart
every bloody day;
you sit there
gluttonously feeding
on the nerves in my brain
and my spine.
The pain is excruciating, true—
physically, mentally, emotionally—
it takes more energy
than I ought to have
to pick myself up, make myself
grit my teeth and carry on.
But I am not going quietly—
you may think you're the boss

but,
for the immediate future
I am in charge here
not you.

Some days I don't have the drive:
days when I know I'm more likely
to climb Everest
than get out of bed.
But, you know what? That's just one day—
I will be back tomorrow.

I know you will win in the end,
but fuck it
you are not going to have it easy.
I am still here—
remember that.

Wonky

You'd be stunned, the times I'm asked,
'You're disabled, how do you…you know?'
How do we make love?
How do we shag?
Well…
slowly,
carefully,
lovingly,
passionately,
kinkily,
dominantly,
submissively,
frenetically…

The list goes on…

We may have to—adapt a bit sometimes,
but, in so many ways,
we're just like you…

What's Best for Him?

I shouldn't be in Amnesty,
I shouldn't be in CAAT,
I should go to the day centre
and maybe weave a raffia mat.

I shouldn't be living on my own,
I should be in a home;
I shouldn't be going out for walks,
I shouldn't be left alone.

I shouldn't be protesting
or writing to my MP;
he's a very busy man you know,
he's got no time for refugees

or equal rights, or anything
I ask him to pursue;
I should be grateful for my P.I.P.
and should tug my forelock too.

I shouldn't be on demos,
I'll bring shame on the family;
can't I just be quietly disabled,
so they can pour out sympathy?

Because though it's sad what's happened
it's all my own fault, you know?
Can't I just accept the charity
and not try to let people know

that the world is up that well-known creek
with neither paddle nor canoe?
Accept the pity, vote Conservative—
that's what they want me to do...

Palliative

This is not a place you leave
unassisted: this is the last
stop before you reach terminus.

It's quiet here: just the gentle whirrs
and clicks of the machinery,
all that's keeping you alive,

sometimes punctuated by
the coughs and wheezings of the patients.
You are one of those patients now.

Bedlinen, starched and gleaming white
a counterpoint to your pallor,
sunken cheeks, fighting for each breath;

I think that you know I'm here:
I squeeze your hand, you nod,
as if to say, 'thank you for being here'.

Speech is gone, so I just sit,
giving you comfort. We both know
the end is not far away.

In memory of Ivor Stanley Moss, 12/8/1908-18/8/2005

Hard Times Happen

If asked, I say, 'Yeah, I'm OK,'
as I don't know what you would say
if I told you the truth, I get
hard times too, I do get upset

scared, down, and lonely: sometimes I
feel so broken I could cry.
I wish I could tell someone how
broken I'm feeling; also how

to help, to support me, to engage—
for now, it's only words on a page.
I can listen to you and that's fine,
but I cannot simply tell you mine.

Please don't think this is about trust,
I don't need to "man up", it's just
I don't want to terrify you
or make you worry that I'd do

something stupid. I will get through
this bad patch—with support from you.
I only need to get my head right,
out of the darkness, into the light.

This Much I Know

This much I know, when your time's running out
you have two choices—you can sulk and pout,
scream about the unfairness of it all,
or stiffen those sinews and say
'Balls to it'—I have had a bloody good life,
tried to help, tried to mitigate strife.
I've met great folks I'm proud to call my friends,
they will still be here when my story ends.

Looking back—is not really for me.
Occasional backward glances, to see
how far I've come; while the path ahead
intrigues me—don't know where it will lead.
I could mourn all those wasted chances,
but I'm on the clock—disease advances.
I do not know quite how long I've got left:
I know loved ones may be feeling bereft

but please don't—we all have our given time,
others want to call on it—but it's mine,
and I've enjoyed it, so hear what I say:
do your best to enjoy every day.
There will be setbacks, that is a given,
tell those who cause them that they're forgiven.
Fix your eyes front, keep those eyes on the prize,
you can bloody do this, you know: surprise

the doubters, surprise yourself! You're amazing,
you've got the power, now let your heart sing!
Keep on, even when you're scared and it's tough—
no matter what they say, you ARE good enough.
In fact, you're better—you're strong, and you care,
you can do things no one else would dare.
So fight the fear, and pick up the baton:
one request—don't forget me when I've gone.

I'm Sorry

I'm sorry we couldn't do more.
I'm sorry we had to keep you
in hospital, restrain you, give
you drugs you didn't want to take.

I'm sorry you hated the staff;
thought of us as prison guards,
whose only joy was stopping you
from doing what you wanted to do.

I'm sorry that the staffing cuts
meant we couldn't give you the time
you needed, meant you thought we didn't
care—we did, and that really hurt.

I'm sorry that we couldn't stop
the voices, the horrific thoughts
you had; the constant urges to cut;
the memories; the flashbacks.

I'm sorry we couldn't make it
all just go away—that there
was so little we could do to help.
I'm sorry it ended this way.

I See Your Scars

No, don't worry,
they're well-hidden
unless—like me—
you know what you're looking for.

I see your scars
reflected in
that thousand-yard stare
I sometimes see
in your beautiful eyes.

I see your scars:
where you had to release the pressure
or you would explode
from the abuse,
the violence,
the bullying, the belittling,
the self-hatred.

From when you were pilloried
about how you look,
your attitude,
your sexuality—
for being you.

I see your scars
and I tell you this:
they are not a sign
of weakness
or failure.

I see your scars
and I see a warrior,
a winner—

someone who has made it through.

I see your scars.
they are part
of your beauty.

Five Deep Breaths

I should be happy now—
sorted some serious stressors—
but I'm—not?
Sinews straining,
body complaining
at the 'fight or flight',
ready to take fright
at the slightest shadow,
or—oh God—
what's that noise?

Stop.

Five deep breaths.
——
——
——
——

I can feel my heart-rate slowing,
the peace that comes from knowing
that—if nothing else
I'm safe.
I may only be at the bottom
of Maslow's pyramid,
but right now—
that's all I need.
I can do more tomorrow.

The Warrior

A museum—somewhere:
their prize exhibit
an ancient warrior's skeleton.
She slips into the museum
late one weekday afternoon
to pay her respects.

A skeleton
smaller than her
with a huge broadsword
lying upon its ribs.
The eyeless, lidless sockets
seem to mock her—
try to make her feel inferior
for not being
a warrior,
a hero.

She sits and thinks on this.
she's not a hero—
but a disabled girl,
who can no more wield that sword
than she could fly to the moon.
That being said
what she is, is a healer,
a carer, a conciliator.
Someone who wants to help,
not to harm.

The Day Before

I was—lucky, I guess:
I got to see you
the day before you died.
You were at home
in a hospital bed,
like a baby in a cot.
You couldn't speak—
you were too far gone—
but I remember
holding your hand
and seeing the recognition
in your eyes.
A smile lit up your face,
you knew who I was,
you knew I was there,
and, believe me,
that made a hell of a difference.
I said goodbye silently,
as I knew
in my heart
this would be
the last time
I saw you.

In memory of Kenneth Edwin Couper, 27/10/1935—30/05/2020

You Held My Hand

You held my hand—doesn't sound much,
but trust me, the power of touch—
especially when you cannot see—
made a huge difference to me.

You held my hand; you knew my name;
used it when you came back again.
It made me feel you really cared,
when otherwise I'd have been scared.

You held my hand, you reassured
when I was feeling insecure.
I felt the calm, I felt the care,
and all from you just being there.

Evolution

Times are strange—
we've had to evolve, to change
to rearrange
the way we care.
But one thing's for sure—
at the heart, the core
of everything we do
is you.
You're not a 'patient', a 'client',
a 'service user';
you're an individual, a person
with hopes, fears, dreams of your own.
And although we've had to
change what we do, and how,
each of us knows
what to do
and we will do that—for you.
The way we do things may have changed,
but our care for you, that's still the same.

We don't want to be Amazing

We don't want to be 'amazing',
we're not here to be inspiration porn,
I know you mean well—but honestly
we're fed up with being used, suborned,
to fit the current fantasy
of the deserving, wretched, poor.

We don't want to be 'amazing',
we'd actually like a normal life
that's not measured out in pills and tablets
but one where we can do what we like
without worrying about the access,
or the braying ableist twats
who think it's 'edgy' to call us 'cripples'—
so original, no one's ever done that…

We don't want to be 'amazing',
we've had enough of being 'brave'.
If we are honest a return to what
we were is what we really crave.
It's flattering to be an 'inspiration'
but the reality is cack—
we'd sign contracts with a demon
if we could get our old lives back.

Priority Seating

Priority seating
on the bus,
represented by a picture,
a stick figure—with a stick.
He uses a stick...

Priority seating,
lots of comforting signs,
'Please give up this seat
for the elderly and less able.'
He's not old.
He's not that old...

Priority seating,
well-intentioned, yes—
but is it just another way
of othering those of us
who are a bit different?
Does he like the idea? Hell, no!
Does he use the seats? Hell yeah...

Battle Royale

So, here we are again—
once more, my nemesis and I
lock horns in combat.
Me, the disabled warrior—damaged yet determined,
you, the king-size bed
with a fitted sheet in need of changing...

Our first skirmish—removing top sheet and pillows—
I win easily, not even breaking sweat,
but now the true contest starts...

I make a dart for the nearest corner of the sheet.
It comes away easily enough,
but this is a mere feint on your part
as I get whacked in the face
by an errant mattress protector
whilst going for the next two corners...

Finally, the old fitted sheet comes off!
It's been a struggle
but I'm still on my feet—just.
Now for the hard part...

I sprawl sideways across the massive mattress,
hands desperately trying, scrabbling
to get that first corner into place.
You don't give up easily though—
as I raise the mattress corner slightly too high
you fight back,
flinging me off yourself
as if I were no more
than a child's teddy bear.
I'm sure I hear you chuckle...

I return to the fray, efforts redoubled:
it's a long, hard, fight
for what seems like hours,
with you doing all in your power
to best me. It matters not.
Finally, the last corner of the sheet
is pulled tight, encasing you.
I win.

I stand, battered, bloodied, yet unbowed.
Once again, I win this gladiatorial bout
against a worthy adversary.
I look upon my handiwork
and think to myself (not for the first time)
I really must get a cleaner...

Excelsior!

Back when I was young
(a long time ago now!)
I guess I took for granted
how many superheroes
had a disability...

Tony Stark and his atomic heart;
Daredevil—the man without fear
was also without sight;
and Professor Xavier,
the leader of the X-Men,
was a wheelchair user.

This kind of normalised
disability for me,
so when I re-read them now
it makes me feel
maybe I could be
a superhero too?

Marvel's disabled warriors—
inspiration.

The Swan

A swan.
What you see:
beauty and elegance, serenely gliding
along the waterway.
What you don't see:
legs paddling away like buggery…

Me.
What you see:
someone doing alright,
coping in spite of the MS.
What you don't see:
pain, constant pain;
fatigue;
the continued pushing above and beyond
to convince myself
that I'm good enough;
the crippling self-doubt;
the wish that
every day didn't have to be like this;
the certain knowledge
that every day will be.

Wabi-sabi

Wabi-sabi.
A Japanese idea,
focused on finding the beauty
within life's imperfections,
accepting peacefully
the cycle of growth and decay.

To some, she may be 'imperfect',
broken, not whole:
but that's their opinion.

At this time
she is able to accept herself
for who she is,
what she is,
finding beauty in imperfection.

To some, she may be decaying,
But she knows
she continues growing.

Stupid Antibodies

For a reason I can't fathom
my antibodies have decided
to stop doing what they're supposed to do
and are now eating me instead...

Instead of eating bugs and lurgies
they have decided that
my nerve fibres would somehow
make a very tasty snack.

They're chewing through the myelin—
like Pac-Man inside of me!
You've no idea how much I wish
for sensible antibodies...

Every day, every hour,
my nerves are under attack:
they're chomping away incessantly
from breakfast to tea—and back.

And so, just to summarise,
as I hope you plainly see,
for some reason it would appear
I've got stupid antibodies!

The House

It's an oldish house—
nothing fancy—
from the outside
it looks in fairly good order.
Once the surveyor's had a look though—
lots of indrawn breaths,
raised eyebrows amongst the tradespeople:
'not going to be a quick job this, squire…'

Do you exercise caution
and leave well alone,
or—do you put the huge amount
of time and effort in?
Decisions, decisions…

Accidental Porn Star

It's come to pass (not quite sure how)
that I'm an accidental porn star now…
I'm not the plumber in a dirty movie,
but 'inspiration porn' you see constantly
on social media and glossy magazines—
oh, the ableds, they adore me!
People love showing off their pity,
their allyship, how we inspire them—
they think we're truly amazing!

It is easy for them to do this with me—
white, middle-class, educated you see.
Invisible disability—that's another plus,
from their perspective I'm 'one of us'!
But heaven forfend, what happens when
you look different—not white, middle-class,
you're not 'one of them'?
Then their allyship is replaced by scorn,
it's left unsaid you should not have been born.
You don't fit the photo, you're too different,
was standing by us what they really meant?

Our paper-thin 'allies' need to learn, and learn quick,
that their inspirations are going to stick
together—we're not here to be
divided—we are diversity.

Reviews

Ade Couper's debut collection is as tender as it is brutal. A frank and honest consideration of the words and ways that form who we are, 'Made of Stories' is a wonder of a book formed of narratives deserving of this page time. Not least among these is the poet's own story of a life-changing diagnosis and the ways in which he contends with this. Couper handles this topic with care, providing heartful insights on the disabled body, what it is like to occupy this space, and what it is like to overcome. This is a collection that will touch many readers.

Dr Charley Barnes, lecturer in Creative and Professional Writing; author of 'Lore: Flowers, Folklore, and Footnotes' (Black Pear Press, 2021)

"...for we are all made of stories" Ade tells us in this powerful debut collection. He opens our eyes and wrenches our hearts as we explore our flaws and accept them as our whole, delving into the dark corners of society's psyche we aim to avoid while Ade shines the brightest light of empathy upon them.

The word "stunning" is often overused, so better to acknowledge "The Japanese have a Word for it…" and apply the gold of Kintsugi to life Ade offers with the treasure of his poems."

Leena Batchelor, Worcestershire Poet Laureate 2020-21

"Ade's content warning is very generous as he prepares us to experience something which many are confronted with without warning. The unapologetic attitude of this collection appropriately reflects the unapologetic nature of chronic health conditions and mental health difficulties. Ade Couper has poured out every ounce of fear, grief and pain to share brutal realities. He is admirably considerate towards the reader whilst remaining intolerant to ignorance, turning his own adversity into another's opportunity to learn.

A caring and courageous collection from a caring and courageous human being.

Informative, important, impossible to ignore. Don't turn away, turn the page."

Jemima Hughes, Poet and Author

Thanks

To the Worcestershire LitFest & Fringe for giving me the opportunity to be Worcestershire Poet Laureate; to the poetry community in Worcestershire and beyond for putting up with me, letting me be part of your events, and for taking part in the many events I've organised.

Grateful thanks also to my family and friends for their encouragement, and also to Black Pear Press for their help and assistance in putting this collection together.

Acknowledgements

'Made of Stories', *One Hundred Memories,* Dream Well Writing (2019)
'Hard Times Happen', *Hard Times Happen*, Black Pear Press (2021)

About the Author

Ade Couper was born in Bedfordshire more years ago than he cares to remember…He has spent the last 20 years working in mental health and dementia support, is a former board member of Amnesty International UK and has been an activist for human rights (particularly disability rights) for over 40 years.

Ade was honoured to be chosen as the Worcestershire Poet Laureate for 2021-2022. He has had poems published in five anthologies to date. This is his first individual collection.